General Music Theory

Speech-based model

Michael Andritsopoulos

General
Music Theory

Speech-based model

IDIFONO

"General Music Theory - Speech-based model"
©Michael Andritsopoulos, 2019
©Idifono, 2019

First Published: 2019

ISBN: 978-618-5450-00-7

Cover: Michael Andritsopoulos

IDIFONO Publications
Mavrokordatou 12,
Aigio, 25100
Greece

+30 2107708527
+30 6948480298
https://www.idifono.gr
e-mail: idifono@gmail.com

Michael Andritsopoulos is a composer from Greece. He was born in 1981 and for the time being, he lives and works in Athens. He is a Fellow of London College of Music with an FLCM in Composition Diploma as well as a Diploma in Composition from Greece. His studies contain algorithmic composition, electrical engineering and European Civilization. His compositions have framed a number of documentaries and several theatrical plays by various theater companies and have been performed in many concert halls such as the Athens Concert Hall (Megaron). A lot of his instrumental pieces have been awarded in international competitions. Today he is the artistic director of a conservatory in Athens and works as composition and advanced theory professor as well as a guitar tutor. He is the author of a guitar method called "Guitharmony", a writer of several small novels published in Greek and an inventor.

Contents

Preface

There are countless theoretical musical models and each one presents a specific view of music theory. By the term theory, I don't mean the conventional musical concept but any aspect that the theoretician can have in terms of constructing a coherent musical system. For example, we could consider such a system the counterpoint or traditional harmony, the systems that were invented in the 20th century (serialism, new complexity, aleatorism, etc.) but also the personal way of writing of each composer who was aware of the way they compose. Each of these systems is trying to equip us with a piece of knowledge to help us expressively, to give us tools to better handle our musical expressiveness. They are essentially algorithms that aspire to classify with completeness (partial or broader) our expressive means.

These algorithms have a direct relationship with the goal, which is the completeness of the musical expression. They are imaging methods of our emotional world to a certain degree. This degree depends on whether the algorithm corresponds to the true principles that may govern our emotional world and how we express it through abstract concepts. I certainly do not rule out the possibility of discovering new dimensions in our psyche through the need for expression within a limited and arbitrary algorithm but in this book I hope to be able to cover the problem of finding an algorithm that corresponds to real empirical data in order to provide a unified theoretical basis for expression in every dominant emotion already objectized in the collective social scene.

Traditional harmony has proved its theoretical potential through time. It has been used by millions of composers around the world and has produced satisfactory expressive results in a vast array of creative needs. On the other hand, there is the 12-tone system whose structure aims to find new musical pathways, which however have as a criterion the degree of distancing from the harmonic relations that the traditional harmony established as desirable. In this second case, historically we find that this algorithm filled a gap that the traditional harmony did not foresee and this allowed to explore musical psychic moods that were in a kind of music "isolation". By showing these two examples of musical theoretical algorithms we are confronted with one thought: could there be an algorithm, wide enough and complete to cover every expressive need?

In the "language games" of L. Wittgenstein, we see the philosophical analogy to what we seek, in the case of language. Words represent concepts that do not have a consolidated meaning but a meaning which is revealed through participation in the context of their specific use. For example, the word "key" has a different meaning to an engineer than to a locksmith or a musician. But what is still valid in the previous work of Wittgenstein is that language has the potential to be an imaging method for reality because the relationships of the concepts we deal with should have an analogy with the actual relationships of the objects we refer to. Expanding the above we could say that music has this imaging power and expresses the emotional world (or even some abstract manifestations of our intellect) but the various theories we use to find music theory tools are simply "games" which only partially manage to yield some minimal intersubjective validity. In my opinion, finding a more complete musical language covering the efforts of imaging and the previous musical algorithms is essential and useful as the existence of societies is in itself evidence of the possibility of finding a common ground of communication and at the same time demonstrates the need for us to be understood by others.

These musical algorithms we mentioned have achieved amazing results but only in an indirect way. Music uses notes, their relationships produce musical rhetoric and structures which we theoretically evaluate with scientific criteria. The discovery of the harmonic series helped us to organize the material that emerged through the collective experience and the analysis of many musical works, in a scientific way. What I mean is that the rules of music theory were taught by a teacher to a student and the audience, through their preferences, acted as a statistical filter that later led to an empirical training of aesthetic rules or guidelines. However, when the harmonic series was discovered and through the work of music theorists like P. Hindemith, we found that there is a mathematical consequence between harmonic relations and the musically sought aesthetic results. It seems obvious, but it's not. There is no apparent causal link between the existence of mathematical patterns and psychometric effects through sound. Biology could provide an answer to this conundrum, suggesting that through evolution our auditory perception adapted the intake of mathematical patterns through sound to feelings of graded liking or disliking. While something like this seems perfectly justified as a case, it is not necessary for this book's endeavor as there is a field of human activity that covers our theoretical need to find an intersubjective expressive field with musical imaging capabilities. That is speech!

I noticed the expressive possibilities of speech in terms of its musical qualities and its relations with the depiction of the mental states and the meaning of speech, through my involvement with teaching. Being a professor of music theory for 20 years, I realized that it was easy for my pupils to understand intervals when I correlated them with punctuation marks, a thought that had arisen spontaneously through the way I viewed the musicality of speech. When I finally realized the possible theoretical implications of this case, namely that the punctuation marks relate to intervals in particular, I decided to examine it methodically and conduct experiments. I was surprised when I stumbled across an unexplored world of theoretical relationships between speech and music and decided to explore it to the end, resulting in the General Music Theory (GMT) which I deeply believe is a musical theory that covers all our expressive needs musically, in a melodic and harmonic level and functions as a single and fully enlarged algorithm which covers the expressive potential of all the other theories and that it is also a method of evaluation of their effectiveness. I, therefore, ended up presenting in detail, through a thesis publication, my heuristic method and experiments but in this book, I will try to show practically how one can use this theory as a basis for any musical endeavor. Whether it is a composition or musical performance and analysis, GMT provides all the tools needed so that someone is able to control their material in every musical environment. Speech contains any biological adaptation we have achieved through evolution as humans, i.e. the ability to give musical entities meaning through the utilization of our common acoustic perception. Our feelings and expressive needs were reflected through speech in a common music venue which became the basis for most (if not all) spoken languages. Languages, more or less, have an internal musical consistency with regard to the expression of speech but the argument of proven intersubjectivity of speech constituted a guarantee in the creation of a pan-human musical "game" in which we can have a detailed and graded perception of the emotional dimensions of the meaning of speech as a carrier.

I will then present in detail how speech helps to create general musical rules and tools. In the first part of the presentation, I will refer extensively to melody and then to harmony, expanding both the conceptual content to enclose the already known methods of dealing with them and also providing a new basis, inspired by a radical point of view, to re-engage with these two concepts. Every musician, composer or critic will find in the GMT what they need to cover their theoretical arsenal and see the music more confidently regardless of the degree to which they are proficient. By depositing my personal experience, I can say that as a composer I have felt that I now have a unifying theoretical framework in which all the systems I have been taught and all the things that I have learned during my experiments can be integrated. By connecting the emotions as well as the rhetorical means of speech with a simple and easily manageable musical algorithm, I gained complete control over my material. I hope that the reader will feel the same way when they give to GMT the opportunity to help them in their musical efforts.

Melody

Intervals as meaning carriers

Speech is a vector of two kinds of information at the same time. One type is, of course, the words and by extension the context of phrases, which has been analyzed enough by the linguistic turn in philosophy and by language-related sciences (linguistics, philology) but also by poetry. However, a phrase does not acquire its full meaning if it is not spoken. Speech carries the second type of information which is what we are interested in in this case as it is information that is conveyed to us through the musicality of speech.

If we did not have any musical information through speech, there would be confusion regarding the meaning of each phrase. For example, if someone asks "Are you going to the soccer field on Saturday?" is the musical information that feeds us with knowledge of the meaning of the phrase. Without it, we would not be able to clarify whether the question focuses on who (are you going?), when (are you going on Saturday?), where (are you going to the soccer field?) or the verb (i.e. if you are going?). Also, the way we ask brings a plethora of emotional connotations, which are absent in text in the majority of cases.

I will first present the conclusions that may be drawn from my research on the rhetorical possibilities of intervals. Punctuation marks have a very specific musical function when it comes to constructing a phrase with a specific meaning. We can say that they are directly related to intervals and their correspondence is generally covered by the following chart.

In order to interpret this chart, we must first know what these symbols mean:

M = major,
m = minor,
P = perfect,
↑ = ascending,
↓ = descending

Energy scale (from strong to weak):   ✓ ✓ ✓ ✓

	Full-stop (period)	Semicolon	Comma	Question mark	Exclamation point
2nd m	✓↑ ✓↓	✓↓			
2nd M	✓↓	✓↑	✓↑		
3rd m			✓↑	✓↑ ✓↓	
3rd M			✓↑	✓↑	
4th P	✓↑ ✓↓				
Tritone	✓↓ ✓↑	✓↑	✓↑	✓↑	✓↑
5th P	✓↓			✓↑	✓↑
6th m	✓↓				✓↑
6th M	✓↓				✓↑
7th m		✓↑		✓↑	✓↑
7th M		✓↑		✓↑	✓↑

In the above, we have to take into consideration the accentuation. Accents are always at the end of the interval, and the last note is the meaning carrier. The only exception is "negation" which can be stated by accenting the previous note and can be expressed by any descending interval.

In the case of an exclamation point, the characteristic interval is not necessarily at the end of the sentence but in the accented syllable of the word that interests us to emphasize.

The repetitions of one note in a melodic structure, according to the GMT and the findings of the research, do not give any meaning but they help to form a temporary tonic because repetitions imprint into our acoustic memory a certain pitch for a longer time. Repetitions usually have only a rhythmic effect.

If the intervals refer to a particular pitch, then the melody shows tonal pull, while the dense alternation of such temporary tonal focal points leads to the conceptualization of a structure with atonal characteristics.

It has been observed that phrases are organized around tonal centers and exhibit fractal structures. To make it easier to understand, let's say for example that the speaker formulates phrase A. Within this phrase, the words that the speaker chooses to organize in a hierarchy are classified by pitch height so that there is a significant correlation between the word and the amount of the note that functions as a temporary tonic.

Example of hierarchy in words tonal height in correspondence with the significance of each word within a sentence:

							Saturday?
Are			going		soccer		
	you			to the		field	this

Similarly, a follow-up phrase is structured (phrase B), but if the two phrases have a rhetorical difference, for example, the second is a question and the first is not, then the tonal center of the second sentence tends to be shifted in a similar interval with the punctuation mark.

Let us see how these are useful in practice. We will analyze two melodic phrases and examine the information given to us by our knowledge of what we mentioned above.

Musical phrase A

In bracket 1 we have a small phrase that starts from the tonic and ends at the 3rd creating the rhetorical analogy of the question mark (see the chart above) and in bracket 2 we have the ending at the tonic through a minor 2nd ascending which corresponds to period (full-stop), as we see in the "period" column in the interval chart.

Then we decide to preserve the components of the motif and create a new phrase, which will have its own temporary tonal focal point up a 3rd.

Musical phrase B

Bracket 1 has exactly the same function while 2 ends in a "comma" due to the major 2nd ascending that occurs diatonically within the selected C major tonality.

If we play the phrases sequentially, we will hear the rhetorical references that we have found above but also the fact that the whole 2nd phrase is received as a question in comparison with the first phrase, thus showing the fractal function of the structures.

Microtonicity and micromobility

We will henceforth call the temporary tonal centers as "microtonality" and intervallic variety as "micromobility" whose measure is proportional to the average size of the observed intervals.

The more limited our material is, the more we will be inclined towards simplifying the implementation of our chart. That is, in a purely tonal environment in which our options for changing the temporary tonal center (i.e. microtonality) are predetermined, a simplified micromobility will apply. For example, in the form of a fugue, in the exposition, we are forced to present our theme in the tonic and then move on to the answer in the dominant. In this case, our familiarity with the form will lead us to our adaptation regarding what we consider to be affirmative and what as a question. We will adapt and accept the theme in tonic as an affirmative phrase and the answer will be considered roughly as an answer.

I would point out that because of the fractal-like structure of rhetoric, we must be rigorous in our formulation and always refer to specific structural portions. That is, if we talk about the rhetoric of two phrases then we will refer to the microtonality of each phrase as a whole and then compare them. However, this does not mean that there are no shifts of microtonicity within each sentence, as each word can contain such shifts from what appears to act as a tonic. Likewise, we can use the same analytical tools for macrostructures such as sonata form or a symphony. The perception of time is subjective and in essence, it can be transformed into an equation in which the apparent time (i.e. the feeling we have for the duration of an event) is proportional to the density of information we receive per objective unit of time.

Let us look at some examples for a better understanding of the tools we have mentioned.

Positivity and accuracy of the intervals

The accuracy of the intervals is dependent on the overall intended tonal (pitch) accuracy. The more accurately one maintains the temporary tonal centers (microtonicity) and the purity of intervals, the more positive is the effect of their speech on the listener. When the notes are accurate (i.e. they do not vary their frequency enough to be approached with an accuracy beyond the 1/4 of the tone) the speech acquires a sense of musicality and makes the listener's experience more positive according to the research. In case of such an accurate melodic way of speaking, intervals have a fairly clear definition, i.e. there are no corresponding deviations that make it difficult to distinguish between neighboring intervals. For example, in such a case it is easy to see the positivity of a question from whether the interval that depicts it is major 3rd or minor 3rd.

Positivity, therefore, has to do with the sense of maintaining the accuracy of the music phrase and the extent to which the intervals belong to the commonly accepted categories of joyful, neutral or sad intervals. What seems to be true through the statistics is how positive are the following: major 2nd, major 3rd, perfect 4th, perfect 5th, major 6th, major 7th and negative are: minor 2nd, minor 3rd, the tritone, minor 6th and major 7th. The octave does not seem to produce any particular emotional information.

Here we see examples with different percentages of accuracy of the pitches and intervals that are set as the frame of each sentence:

you heard what hap-pened to my home?

we re-hearsed them, we talked a-bout them,

In the second phrase there are variations of 1/4 in the pitches that have a repeat function rather than a punctuation mark.

The sorting of spaces in discernible categories is not the result of research bias. Based on the samples I collected, it is clear that the behavior of the punctuation marks is not confused with the behavior of repetitions. The former ones have a specific function within the phrase while the latter ones only have an auxiliary role. Therefore, the adoption of microtonal shifts is a distinct phenomenon that relates solely to the accuracy that we wish to achieve in terms of pitch-tone clarity.

It seems that biology has played a role here as well because in order to justify this rough categorization of intervals we should take into account the influence of natural acoustics in the formulation of the music code of speech.

The harmonic series

The harmonic series is a series of intervals that are produced by a fundamental pitch, as harmonics. If we set the fundamental to C then the series is shaped as follows:

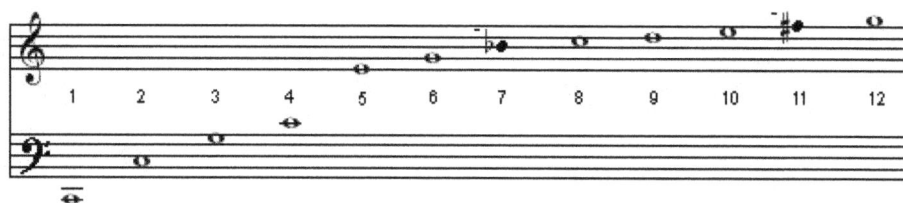

The longer we move away from the 1st harmonic, the harder it is to hear the next one and based on the characteristics of the average ear ability, we conclude that the closest harmonics are the ones that played the most important role in the formation of the speech code. From the 5th to the 8th harmonic it is usually difficult to manage to identify them and the farther we move, the more difficult it gets.

So, if we listen to an interval then it makes sense that it sounds more pleasant if it is in the first harmonics of the fundamental, as evolution, most likely, adapted our preferences with the criterion of necessity and benefit.

The octave, being the first in the list of intervals of the series, gives us only little new information when we hear it. The perfect 5th as a 3rd harmonic brings pleasant feelings.

The first perfect 4th we hear is formed between the 3rd and 4th harmonic i.e. from the 5th to the tonic (second octave) and this explains the tendency to associate this interval with a full-stop. We sense that in the interval of G - C, C is the tonic and that makes it obvious why the perfect 4th ascending is accompanied by a connotation of a full-stop.

In the 5th harmonic we see the major 3rd and this interval is associated with a pleasant feeling of question, according to the index of punctuation marks we've seen previously and of what we discussed in the previous chapter. The 3rd formed between the 5th and 6th harmonic is a minor 3rd and requires more effort to recognize, because it is more distant from the fundamental than the major 3rd we mentioned but also because it is not formed from the tonic but from the 3rd of the fundamental. The E - G interval continues to have a tonal reference to C. Someone would think that the minor 3rd is categorized in speech as a question just like the major 3rd, because it is much closer to it than to other intervals we come across in the first 5 harmonics and so we perceive it as an interval of the same rhetoric but differing in the amount of positivity.

The first interval of a 2nd is found between the 7th and 8th harmonic and is a major 2nd. The 7th harmonic is at the same time a minor 7th above the 4th harmonic which is the tonic as is also the 8th one. All these along with the observation that it is a harmonic very difficult to hear explains why it is considered more as a comma and a semicolon (major 2nd ascending and minor 7th ascending respectively) rather than a full-stop.

Because of the fact that the harmonics beyond the 7th one, are inaccessible to most people, we believe that the intervals of 6th and 7th are to be treated within the code as approaches of nearby intervals such as 5th and 8th respectively. This observation justifies the behavior displayed in the index of punctuation marks.

Melodic line mobility

In the construction of phrases, the approximation of the intervals of the index (of punctuation marks) as well as the preservation of temporary tonal centers (stable microtonicity) is related to positivity. Also related to positivity is the general tendency to widen the intervals, which is also proportional to the level of emotional energy in the projected melodic line.

In the phrases below we see great mobility while we get differentiated amounts of positivity in each case:

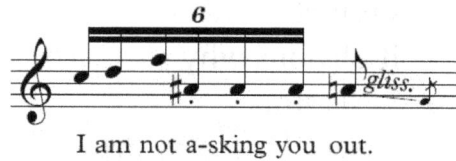

I am not a-sking you out.

ob-vious-ly_____you're not   a gol - fer

In the first one, there is plenty of negativity (the final interval which we encounter in denial is typical) while in the second one we have a phrase slightly playful with cheerful character.

In the case of high-energy negative emotions like anger, we may have some discrete big leaps in the melody which act as temporary tonal stations as they are surrounded by many repetitions (as shown in the first case).

Formalism

Xenakis in his work "Formalized Music" attempted for the first time to set some foundations to the confrontation of music as algorithm and introduced methods that help categorize our priorities on the main and secondary musical elements of any model. And while this way the mathematically possible models that arise are innumerable, speech operates on the basis of 3 basic axes, Energy, Positivity and the Emphasis which in turn act in the formulation of speech through 7 secondary factors, Intensity, Tonal Accuracy, Note separation (whether the notes are distinguishable, glissando - legato - staccato), Vibrato amount, Duration (relative duration based on the enacted as an average duration), Mobility (tendency for steps or leaps) and the frequency of pauses.

The aim of this book is to give the musicians tools for practical use of an algorithm of the totality of music which will allow them to apply it in practice. Consequently, I thought it is important to be able to connect these 7 secondary factors directly related to known concepts of our rhetorical training. Our speech uses these 7 factors to express the emotional content of the meaning of our words and therefore I considered that instead of a non-imprecise and inaccurate function in psychometric terms, it would be advisable to associate them with discrete emotional situations we all know. So, the 3 axes that we mentioned are essentially columns containing 17 known emotions.

I chose these emotions as representative as they are states that are recognized in the international bibliography and at the same time have a strong empirical interest because they are known to us all. They are essentially discrete areas within a system of two axes, Energy and Positivity. The values in between these areas are infinite but it is more practical to present the correlations with these 17 emotions than the abstract relationships of quantities that cannot be accurately measured as they are psychometric subjects.

Let us first look at this system of the two axes where we detect emotions as distinct areas.

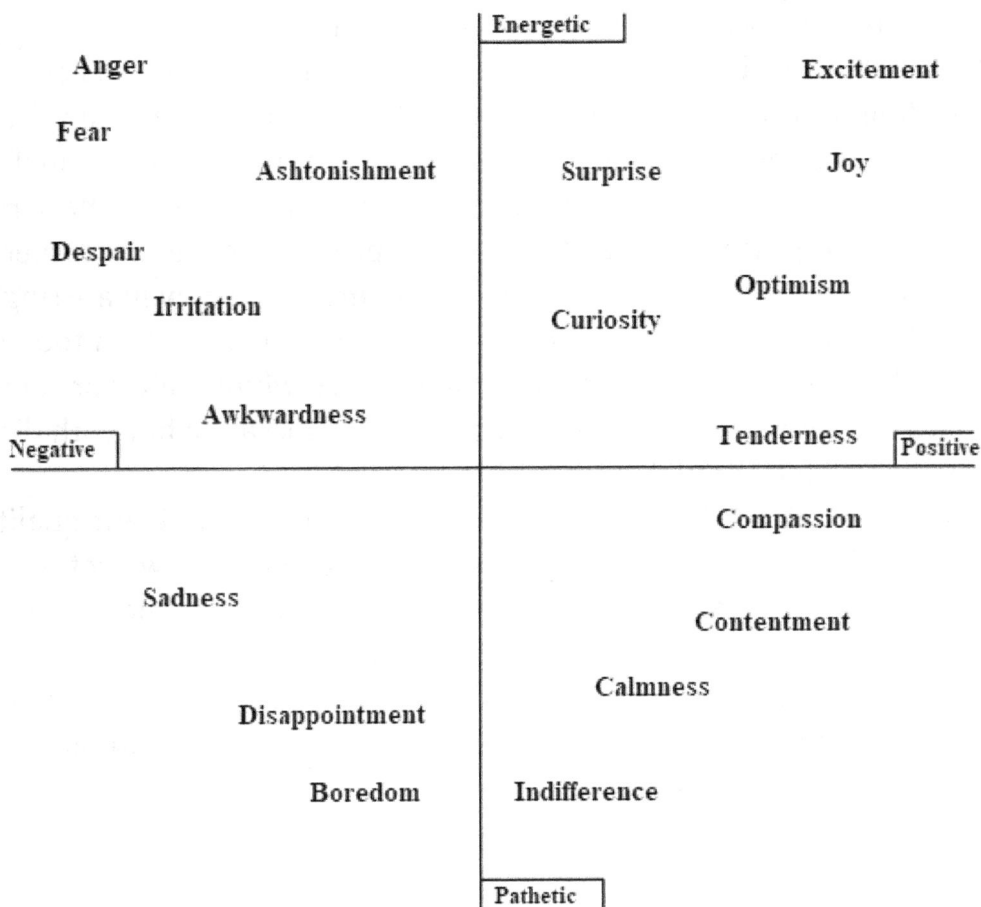

		Energetic		
Anger				Excitement
Fear				
	Ashtonishment		Surprise	Joy
Despair				
	Irritation		Curiosity	Optimism
	Awkwardness			Tenderness
Negative				Positive
				Compassion
Sadness				Contentment
	Disappointment		Calmness	
	Boredom	Indifference		
		Pathetic		

The third axis, the one of Emphasis emerged from the needs of expression and not from the needs of the classification of emotions. The expression through speech differentiates somewhat the manipulation needs of the 7 secondary factors. Let's first see the final form of the speech model and then see how what we learned can transform the way we see music.

First, we will analyze existing melodies which will ensure that they cover as wide an aesthetic range as possible to make it clear that the speech model contains the rhetorical needs of musical expression as a whole. This has proven its empirical base. It's something that seems obvious to me after I familiarized myself with this algorithm. In my view it is clear that if someone accepts the fundamental assumption of my original argument, namely that in the speech there is all that the need for expression embodied by the natural acoustics and that it is the most complete way of illustration of our inner world, then it is a simple logical consequence to accept that the musical components of speech can explain all our aesthetic attempts. Familiarization with the algorithm will provide the musician with the tools to handle any known kind of musical organization and future ways of expression through music.

The sense of "intimacy" is expressed in a particular way. It is connected with providing information on how the sound is produced. For example, it is a sign of intimacy when the sound of the air passing through the channel of our throat is heard as we speak, as we often do when we sigh or puff. The same can be achieved by projecting the way the sound is produced on an instrument (e.g. blowing – aeolian sounds in a woodwind, the sound of the bow in a string, etc.).

In particular, we also need to mention that glissando can be a tool of intimacy as well as it is the main element accompanying whimsicality or complaint (two modes of expression with the same amount of glissando but with different positivity manifested through appropriate intervals).

What we mentioned above in conjunction with the dominant qualities of each emotion (i.e. the values we receive in the 7 columns if we set a specific emotion in the 3 main axes), can be a way of organizing musical material to composition, aid for orchestration (because this will make it easier for us to find relevant qualities in instrument techniques and sound colors) and an analysis tool to judge whether an idea finds a matching expression in a composition and whether a score finds matching performance in an interpretation.

Level	Energy	Positivity	Emphasis
17	Anger	Excitement	Anger
16	Fear	Joy	Irritation
15	Excitement	Optimism	Surprise Ashtonishment
14	Joy	Tenderness	Curiosity
13	Surprise Ashtonishment	Compassion	Tenderness
12	Optimism Despair	Contentment	Compassion
11	Irritation	Surprise	Despair
10	Curiosity	Curiosity	Calmness
9	Awkardness	Calmness	Optimism
8	Tenderness	Indifference	Joy
7	Compassion	Ashtonishment	Contentment
6	Contentment	Boredom	Disappointment Excitement
5	Sadness	Disappointment	Sadness
4	Disappointment	Awkardness	Boredom
3	Calmness	Irritation Anger	Indifference
2	Indifference	Sadness	Awkardness
1	Boredom	Despair Fear	Fear

	Volume	Vibrato	Articulation	Duration	Pitch Accuracy	Mobility	Rest Ratio
17	fff	semitone	staccato	♪	precise tone	frequent leaps	frequent rests
16							
15							
14	ff			♪			
13							
12	f						
11				♪ 6			
10					width of a semitone	necessary leaps only	necessary rests only
9	mf	quartertone	legato				
8				♪			
7	mp						
6							
5				♩			
4	p						
3					width of a whole tone	tendency for repetitions	no rests
2	pp	none	glissando	♩			
1							

tendency to choose these intervals	Positivity	tendency to choose these intervals
minor 2nd, 3rd and 6th		major 2nd, 3rd and 6th
augmented 4th		perfect 4th and 5th
diminished 5th		minor 7th
major 7th		octave

black arrow = proportional   grey arrow = inversely proportional

Concerning information

There is coded information of various levels in speech. While in this book we refer in detail to the musical components of the speech we should mention as a separate study the meaning of the flow of information. The density of information influences the level of interest of the listener. While one realizes very easily that the denser the information the greater the interest of the listener, this is only half (or less than half) true.

In practice, what is being observed is that what is causing the preservation of interest is stability in the rate of change in the flow of information. Interest is caused if we alter the flow of information either positively or negatively. There is certainly no equation that shows the amount of interest as a function of the rate of change in the flow of information (which flow is information/time). It is useful though, to know that the flow of information is another rhetorical element that music has borrowed from speech and we can check and evaluate it adequately.

Information is not limited to the amount of intervals/time or the amount of data/time. These and several more can be controlled indirectly as these musical quantities exist as secondary categories in the 7 columns of our algorithm (e.g. anger as an energetic emotion has a tendency for small rhythmic values and therefore a high density of notes/time). Information may constitute the change of any element (musical quantity) per time. It may involve a change in the pressure of a bow or the change in orchestration etc. Harmony is also a field in which many variations can be made at the level of information because it consists of many simultaneous melodies thus many information carriers.

Finally, the change can occur through the handling of anticipation. When the listener expects something particular due to the fact that there is already an entrenched regularity (of some kind) at a structural level, in the majority of listeners, in the normality of structure of the musical phrases, then any change from the expected has a depending effect in terms of the evaluation of information.

A common acoustic bias is symmetry. If symmetry is disturbed then interest is caused. Interest can cause negativity or positivity depending on the flexibility of the listener's adaptation (which has cultural components associated with extensions on psychology).

If a musical object A is equal to B (let's say we refer to the size of phrases in bars) then it is expected that after a repetition of A, we expect B unchanged. But if B differentiates and becomes B'>B, then the extra portion (i.e. the B'-B) will be the subject of attention, it will be projected onto our attention. If the opposite happens, that is to say, B'<B, then our expectation towards what follows will be intensified.

Let's see some applications of the algorithm in the analysis of music extracts and in composition.

● ● ● ● ● ● ● ●

Analysis

We will see how the model of GMT can evaluate the aesthetic content and the rhetorical elements of the melodies that we will choose.

1. *Clair de lune* – C. Debussy
extract from the theme melody

We will try a review of the aesthetic content of the extract by making references and correlations to the 7 secondary musical quantities of the algorithm of our speech model, so that we can then draw conclusions about the emotional effect that is caused to the listener through the quantities relations of what we will spot, in reference with the 3 primary axes of the model. In other words, we'll try to identify with precision what the musical subject which is trying to communicate with the listener, is trying to convey.

Volume: approximately 3 or 4 in the volume columns values.

This implies that since Volume is proportional to Energy and Emphasis, some possible feelings that are caused to us are the following: Calmness, Frustration, Indifference, and Boredom (i.e. emotions with values of 3 or 4 in their respective axes).

Vibrato: Since it was written for piano, we would say that Vibrato is at its minimum value.

The column of Vibrato is inversely proportional to the axis of Positivity, which hikes the value we receive on that axis at number 17, that is, in Joy or Optimism.

Articulation: legato dominates. This means average values in this column.

This leads to average values in Positivity and Emphasis, where emotions such as Tranquility, Optimism, Joy, and Indifference are found.

Duration: Average duration.

Duration is proportional to the Energy and inversely proportional to the Emphasis. As we speak of average values, we receive the following feelings: Tenderness, Awkwardness, and Optimism, Joy respectively. Again, we have the same overlapping in Optimism and Joy.

Pitch accuracy: We get the ultimate precision as the piano produces only precise tones.

So high values in this column mean correspondingly high values in the axis of Positivity, which refers to the emotions of Joy, Optimism, and Excitement.

Mobility: We generally observe steps and only a few leaps.

The frequency of the small intervals means average values for the Mobility column so, Calmness, Curiosity, Indifference are the emotions we get respectively from the values in the axis of Positivity.

Rest rate: absence of rests (the first rest does not create an effect as there are no notes preceding).

This column is inversely proportional to Positivity, so we receive the values of Joy, Optimism, and Excitement. It is proportional to the Emphasis axis, so it predisposes us for Fear, Awkwardness, and Indifference.

Flow of information: sparse at the beginning and denser as it goes. Information here identifies with the duration of the notes along with the choice of intervals. Since these two have been reported as Duration and Mobility, we will not refer to the flow of information separately.

Taking into account all these indications, we would say that the emotional component of our theme refers to feelings that are cheerful and optimistic (which highlights also the scale which as a major scale leads to an increase in the general sense of Positivity). At the same time, however, we receive a latent sense of indifference which, in combination with the general positivity, is perceived as a stochastic disposition with a dose of tenderness.

The octave with which the theme begins projects energy which is not supported afterwards as a descending melodic path follows, moving from the superficial enthusiasm of the beginning to an increasingly greater innerness.

The leaps that occur sparingly in the melodic line, which generally consist of steps, create small stops, sometimes affirmative ones and sometimes interrogative ones, but only to be quickly passed and lost in the flow of inner reflection. The endings of the phrases are affirmative but not by the strongest kind (descending 2nd in bars 2, 4, 6 and 8, at the end of the phrases marked with legato lines).

It is, therefore, a quiet, cheerful melody that stands between detachment and tenderness, which begins with some relative excitement and ends more thoughtfully, almost melancholic in an overall innerness impression.

2. *Pierrot Lunaire* - Arnold Shoenberg
extract from the voice line

Ge _ lü _ ste,   schau _ er _ lich und

süß ____,   durch _ schwimmen oh_ne Zahl   die   Flu _ _ _ ten!

(Publisher Info. Vienna: Universal Edition, 1914, Plate U.E. 5334, Reprinted info Mineola: Dover Publications, 1994)

27

The tempo indication is: **Bewegt** (♩ ca 66 – 76) which, as a directive, encourages a very emotional interpretation. The tempo is relatively slow but the rhythm of the passage focuses on the 16th notes and that makes it fast. The mobility of the melody is wide. The Articulation is great (absence of legati and glissandi). The tension as we see from the prior noted dynamic (not shown in the excerpt) is p and pp. The elaborated atonic structure suggests a low level in positivity because of the fact that atonal music tries to avoid intervals that relate to known tonal structures thus pleasant intervals from the first five harmonics of the harmonic series. No vibrato observed. There are no rests that interfere with the melody. The Pitch accuracy is low as there is the indication "Gesprochen" that shows the singer not to be accurate in pitches so to remind more of speech than singing.

If we do a similar procedure to the one we followed in "Clair de Lune", we will find out how the elements we find above refer to specific emotions in the 3 axes.

The intervals which the composer uses to organize the melodic line have an interesting variety. However, the points of the endings of the phrases in measures 4 and 6, in which we see the repetition of the interval E – C# descending, are of particular efficacy. This is the most characteristic interval of negation, which is consistent with the actual dimension of the situation of the subject's psychology (the singer).

Small values along with low Positivity and low dynamics indicate Fear. Low Positivity is manifested by low Pitch accuracy. On the other hand, the absence of rests and increased Mobility are contradictory to the former findings. To express Fear, there is a strong element of the falter, i.e. frequent pauses. Also accompanied by very low Mobility, we would say that the repetition of notes, rather than variety, dominates. So, what does the combination of the above produce? Exactly what the composer wanted to achieve, a contradiction in the expression that informs us of similar internal contradictions of the psychism of the subject (the character who is impersonated by the singer). Madness arises from these contradictions. This is consistent with the aspirations of the text of the symbolist Albert Giraud, who found the appropriate expression through the expressionistic style of composing of A. Shoenberg.

3. *Violin concerto 1* - Karol Szymanowski

(Editor: Paul Kochanski cadenza and violin part First edition, Publisher Info. Vienna: Universal Edition, 1923. Plate U.E. 7260)

Since we have shown how we can approach a musical text quite in detail in the previous examples, at this point it would be a good idea to show how we can quickly focus on the dominant features of a musical text to easily get conclusions about its emotional content.

In the excerpt above we see small rhythmic values (it's a quick passage) and strong dynamics. These features predispose us to high values in the Energy axis. Seeing the table of two axes (Energy-Positivity) we can easily reject any emotions that are not above the horizontal axis as we need to look at the most energetic emotions in our system. Anger, Fear, Joy, Frustration, Surprise, Astonishment, Excitement, Despair, and Optimism are the most likely to represent this passage.

The melodic movement shows signs of low mobility (small intervals) with abrupt transitions through leaps to other microtonicities. This is characteristic of Anger, for example, more than it is Fear's, whose distinct difference from anger is Volume (low dynamics). We reject the case that positive emotions are projected due to the chromaticity of the score. The final confirmation that it is an "angry" sounding passage is given by the staccati and tenuti who declare message clarity (in anger we seek to make clear what we mean, unlike fear who overwhelms us and does not help us articulate well) as well as the accents that produce small bursts of dynamics. The trills also give evidence of negativity as they have the same effect as a vibrato of some greater range, which also targets Anger. One would notice that it would suffice just to hear the passage to draw the conclusion that it is an "angry" passage, but let's remember the purpose of knowing the algorithm, which is to gain control over our material. Knowing the way the algorithm works, will give us the advantage to achieve desirable results on the basis of our theoretical tools, we will know which technical aspects affect the emotional components that we seek to produce and we'll have a full understanding over analysis issues.

In this case, we attempt a critical evaluation and we see whether such a performance attributes all these traits of Anger, which is the emotion the composer wanted to produce. As music teachers, we can direct a new student with absolute knowledge of the technical aspects that need the student's attention for every score whose emotional orientation we are able to know or track through the GMT. Even more so, in the case of a new composer, through the practice with the algorithm of the GMT, he/she develops the critical ability to know whether the desired result is consistent with the method followed.

4. *Pression* – Helmut Lachelmann

Excerpt from the score.

The work is written for cello. In the particular notation of the score, only the actions of the performer on the instrument are marked and not notes.

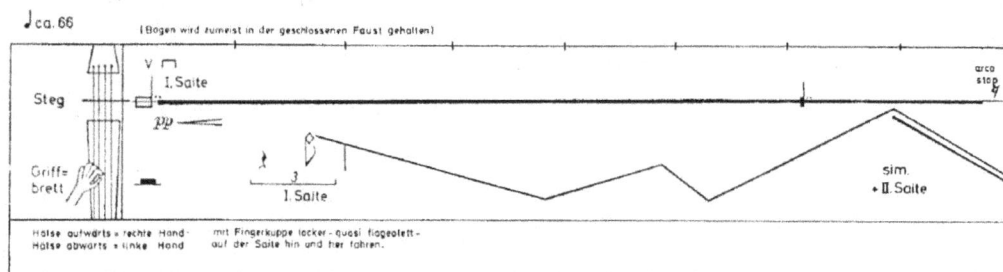

(Breitkopf @ Härtel, Wiesbaden – Leipzig – Paris)

In the excerpt, we see that our information is limited down to only a few elements. The movement of the left hand, in essence, produces only noise and not specific notes. The change in flow, i.e. the perceived speed of noise, is created through the largest or smallest displacement of the left hand as it is drawn on the strings in relation to the time that each movement lasts. All our attention is focused on this element which, due to our limitation in terms of information, is forced to focus on any flow of information, albeit small.

This noise causes our direct information about the way the sound is produced on the cello, while the bow produces a stable result with the sole differentiation of a crescendo. This information is riveting because of the intimacy brought by immediacy.

The same is observed many times in intense string instrument phrases. Due to the technique (e.g. spiccato), apart from the notes we also hear the noise of the bow's friction which is consistent with agitation in performance because Anger can be easily combined with audacity. This happens because audacity provides an expression that defies any detachment due to kindness and passes easily to a rude intimacy (revealing information that would otherwise have been concealed, such as the way the sound was produced – let us think in analogy the disturbing sounds of the oral cavity escaping from the careless speaker).

Using the algorithm we can easily justify the differences between musical genres.

For example, the difference between technique and romance is by definition in positivity because of the philosophy that governs each system in choosing its tonal material. The absence of tonality sets the serialism towards the negative values of the Positivity axis as it alienates the listener from the possibility of anticipating the melodic action (like the use of scale or other tonal structures would offer), creating an inability to trace the microtonicity which leads to corresponding inability to recognize punctuation and other rhetoric elements associated with the use of temporary tonal centers in speech. This phenomenon is perceived negatively as it matches the sense of loss of the "center" of the personality, as is the case of the confused, desperate speech.

Among genres and subgenres, the palette of emotions can also easily be traced. In this case, differences are limited and so we can easily predict the effect of each variation. A typical example is in the field of metal music among the genres: death and thrash, where the main difference is that in the first genre the vocals belong to the technique "growl" where there isn't a clear singing but more of a rhythmic recitation with distortion of the voice timbre and the second genre has more typical vocals, singing with a clear timbre. The effect that will be caused by this variation is easy to predict. As we see in the GMT algorithm, the variable affected is mainly the Pitch accuracy. The vast differentiation of one genre to the other in Pitch accuracy has a direct and predictable acoustic effect. If we consider the genre with the clear vocals as "normal"(thrash), then in the column of Pitch accuracy we move from the highest value to the lowest one when we switch to "death" genre. This is directly related (it is proportional) to the magnitude of Positivity as shown by the algorithm and if we observe the emotions that exist at the lowest values of this axis, that this difference forces us to move to, we will see Irritation, Anger, Sadness, Despair, and Fear. It is clear, therefore, that by making a variation, we can easily see the effect that this choice may have, in terms of handling the projected emotion rhetorically.

The change in the average flow of information is also an easy way to draw conclusions about the characteristics of musical genres. For example, in my opinion, and completely subjectively speaking, the flow of information in most jazz tracks can be characterized denser than the one we encounter in fusion music. The complexity of harmony may be similar but the harmonic pace is most often slower in fusion (no matter how fast or slow someone plays in improvisation). This also captures a change in the normality of the emotional motifs that characterize each idiom, often making jazz music a subject of criticism with many listeners feeling overwhelmed by information while experimental fusion harmonies with fewer chords per time unit seem more easily accepted by non-expert audience.

But we will say more about harmony in the corresponding chapter that will follow.

.

● ● ● ● ● ● ● ●

Synthesis

We will try to make some examples to understand how we can use the algorithm so we can make our own melodies in a way that allows for total control of our rhetoric.

Starting out, we will create a pattern based on some rhetorical guidelines that we will set out as a desideratum (our goal). Then we will make variations by changing elements based on the 7 columns of the algorithm and the punctuation marks, so as to monitor how the pattern affects these changes.

Motif and variations

We pre-defined the level of Pitch accuracy and established a level of Positivity choosing in advance to create a pattern within the tonal appropriation. Notes can be drawn from a scale or there can be chromatic notes but there is a given accuracy of each tone in this case. Without accompaniment, this motif can work with a plethora of possible harmonizations, which we will not take into account. So, we have narrowed the field in which the values for the 7 columns can be differentiated as in practice some aesthetic decisions we make as we compose, are made before we even touch the pen on paper.

In the original motif we decided that we want something of medium Energy and high Positivity to exude something Optimistic and Tender. These influenced the Volume, Duration, Mobility and the Rest rate as these are the quantities whose values we had not pre-decided, while the Vibrato and the Articulation were left unchanged (zero in each case). In terms of the rhetoric of punctuation, we begin by moving from A to B, creating a comma, then doing the same from the B to C# (repetitions of the notes as we have mentioned only have a rhythmic role). The couple C# - A looks like a temporary negation which, however, immediately gives way to an exclamation mark through the transition from A to E. Finally, we have an ending by the connection of a descending 2nd (which is the 3rd of the scale and it involves the feeling of half cadence or a question mark according to GMT, but since we have no harmony underlying, this feeling remains latent).

Original motif

Let us try to make it more Positive, namely to move more decisively towards Optimism, Joy and Excitement. We will alter mobility and where we have the unvarying repetitions we will introduce question marks which give a playful feel (A - C#, B - D) instead. At the same time, we will also raise the Articulation and, where we have no relative indications, we will introduce some points with staccato which also relate to Positivity. Even though Articulation is related proportionally to the Emphasis and negative emotions are that high on the axis, nevertheless, Positivity is assured by the choices we took at the beginning regarding the scale (this is a major scale). Therefore, by increasing the Articulation to something already positive, one raises, even more, the positivity as the message becomes clearer through greater articulation. The small rhythmic values that help to lead the notes that are common with the original motif give a shift in the average Duration column, making the passage faster and thus more energetic while diminishing Emphasis by returning the values to this axis back to the average values.

Then we tried to change it a lot and make it project timid feeling. Characteristics to be emphasized in this case are the rate of Rests, the low Volume and the low Pitch accuracy associated with the axis of Emphasis as well as the quicker rhythm. From the Positivity axis-related quantities we changed Mobility, greatly reducing it through the preference of neighboring notes instead of leaps. In regard to the rhetoric related to punctuation, we changed the ending in a distinct way, resulting more conservatively back into the microtonicity center, so as not to widen the extent of the melody range to the previous proportions.

We conclude that it is easy to familiarize ourselves with the algorithm of the GMT by influencing a few or even a single factor in every change we make so that we learn, one step at a time, how to handle all the columns of the algorithm at will and in combinations. Below we will see an excerpt from a quartet of mine in which I do exactly that, I only alter one factor.

There is a motif of 4th notes which makes its appearance successively on the cello, the 1st violin and then on the 2nd violin. With the help of OpenMusic software, I was able to calculate the percentage by which I increase the Mobility of this motif, varying the intervals between the notes in order to raise the value of the Mobility column. This axis is related to Positivity and the intended result was to move progressively towards Excitement, which we perceive when we hear the passage.

Full theme

Now we will try to reduce restrictions to give an example of a composition in a quite enlarged harmonic environment, almost undetermined (at least it was not our intention to pre-define it). Our goal will be to target the various emotions that we want to display in every phrase. Instrumentation and any rhetoric related to any restriction imposed by it (e.g. extent and technical capabilities of the institution) will be the only pre-determined factors.

So let us say that we want a rhetoric that shows the following passages:

At first, we have Calmness, suddenly there is a Surprise and it gradually goes towards Disappointment. Then return to Calmness with some hints of Optimism.

These, of course, determine direct factors from the columns of our model, such as Duration, Rest rate, Volume, Articulation and Pitch accuracy, Vibrato and Mobility. But the question of where to put the tonal centers (microtonicity focal points) that we mentioned earlier has not been solved yet.

It is necessary to link the concept of orchestration as the instruments have other possibilities than the voice. Voice selects these centers based on its overall range.

This works adequately due to the phenomenon of the spectral displacement of timbre, thus creating the psycho-acoustic phenomenon of the immediate uptake of the energy state of the expression of speech in relation to the relative tonal height (as the voice reveals its energy through the difficulty of achieving the highest pitches, which is a common experience among speakers and listeners).

Regarding instruments, this is not always the case. For example, the strings have a relatively similar ease of producing notes in the totality of their tonal range, so this sensation will not be effectively rendered. But in woodwinds, it is easier to feel this difference in the effort of producing various pitches as it depends a bit on the blowing intensity that carries an analogy with the difficulty mentioned above. In keyboard instruments, there is an almost absolute uniformity in the difficulty of accessing and rendering the total range of the instrument. Therefore, in instruments that this parameter is not evident, energy-related elements will more actively accompany these shifts from one tonal center to another, in order to create the requested emotional tension through the appropriate combination. The various techniques that can be applied to the instruments are very useful at this point and so is the knowledge for the diagram of the volume of the notes in relation to the tonal height (as this is not always linear).

So let us set a modest range for all the notes we have at our disposal, so that we can see how we will apply our thoughts to different instruments and define on this basis our tonal centers in relation to the rhetoric we have chosen by examining at the same time the possibilities of different instruments per range (we will use indicatively the violin and the flute).

Let's define the total available range:

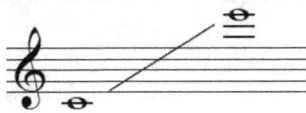

In the case of the violin, this range shows uniform characteristics, so we do not limit the nature of the instrument to affect the proportions we get through the model.

In the case of flute, this range does not have uniformity and changes according to the area in the way we will see in the image below[1]:

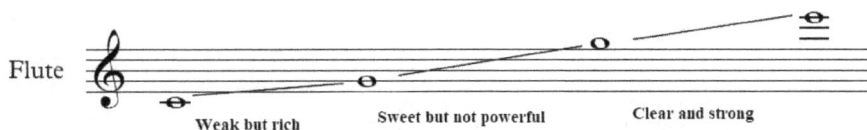

Flute

Weak but rich   Sweet but not powerful   Clear and strong

So let's choose original values from the model in relation to the rhetoric we chose, in the case of a violin orchestration:

---

1. According to information from the book "The Study of Orchestration" by Samuel Adler.

Calmness

Volume	Vibrato	Articulation	Duration	Pitch Accuracy	Mobility	Rest Rate
p	minimum	legato	♩	semitone width	Necessary leaps	necessary rests

Estimated microtonicity: Vln.

Surprise

Volume	Vibrato	Articulation	Duration	Pitch Accuracy	Mobility	Rest Rate
ff	average	close to staccato	♪ (6)	semitone width	tendency for leaps	necessary rests

Estimated microtonicity: Vln.

Disappointment

Volume	Vibrato	Articulation	Duration	Pitch Accuracy	Mobility	Rest Rate
mp	plenty	close to glissando	♪	width of less than a whole tone	tendency for repetitions	frequent rests

Estimated microtonicity: Vln.

Optimism

Volume	Vibrato	Articulation	Duration	Pitch Accuracy	Mobility	Rest Rate
mf	plenty	close to staccato	♪	precision	tendency for leaps	necessary rests

Estimated microtonicity: Vln.

Now that these have been established, the only thing that remains is their application in order to create a theme with this particular rhetoric. In this effort, we will take into consideration the general conclusions we mentioned in the previous chapter and the tendency for positive or negative intervals. The latter will be taken into consideration in conjunction with the index of punctuation marks so that there is control of melody's overall rhetoric.

In the score above we have put in exaggeration some elements to show clearly our intentions. In a theme, which has only one emotional disposition rather than many as the theme above, it is easier to understand alterations by changing only some of the factors we examined with a tendency of small shifts in our main axes and therefore to control the rhetoric per phrase. For example, if we increase the average Duration, we increase the Emphasis, if we increase the Volume, we increase the Energy too and so on. This way we can control the impact that any change of these quantities has over the emotional content of the theme. We always refer to the emotional shifts regardless of the subjective perception. We are talking about the commonplace of emotional communication that we have examined through the expression of speech and which is the only objective way to handle what is used to transmit information concerning emotion among people.

*
h.p. = high bow pressure
n.p. = normal bow pressure
l.p. = low bow pressure

The fact that the flute has an uneven distribution of the various qualities of its timbre and its overall capabilities, in this range, leads us to use adjustments to related quantities (as provided by the model), in certain areas of the range, to achieve the same effectiveness as the violin in the rhetoric we set.

So the indexes concerning the violin in relation to the emotion we set, will now be shaped as follows:

Calmness

Volume	Vibrato	Articulation	Duration	Pitch Accuracy	Mobility	Rest Rate
mp	minimum	legato	♩	semitone width	necessary leaps	necessary rests

Estimated microtonicity: Fl.

Surprise

Volume	Vibrato	Articulation	Duration	Pitch Accuracy	Mobility	Rest Rate
mf	average	towards staccato	♪	semitone width	tendency for leaps	necessary rests

Estimated microtonicity: Fl.

Disappointment

Volume	Vibrato	Articulation	Duration	Pitch Accuracy	Mobility	Rest Rate
mp	plenty	towards glissando	♪	width of less than a whole tone	tendency for repetitions	frequent rests

Estimated microtonicity: Fl.

Optimism

Volume	Vibrato	Articulation	Duration	Pitch Accuracy	Mobility	Rest Rate
mp	plenty	towards staccato	♪	precision	tendency for leaps	necessary rests

Estimated microtonicity: Fl.

It can be noted that we have only transformed the volume and tonal centers considering the volume in the respective areas.

*
flz = flutter tongue

Some techniques were adapted as expected. The result is equally convincing. We hope that the readers will try playing them to find out for themselves.

In the following example, an attempt was made to accompany the melody above. The instrument we chose is the piano because of the uniformity of the timbre and volume in its entire range.

flz = flutter tongue

43

The tempo does not need to be specific, the axes act as interdependent quantity indexes, so the Energy of the whole subject will be less than another with a faster tempo, but all the factors of the model are interdependent and thus they affect proportionally the result.

As for the accompaniment of the piano, harmony emerged through thoughts that we will analyze in the next chapter.

Harmony

If we consider the chord as every consonance of notes, the rhetoric of the succession of chords (progression) will be associated with the rhetoric of the melodic movement of each note. The chord is only an intermediate condition from the minimal harmonic environment which is a single note, to the maximum which contains all available notes.

While in the first section of the book we analyzed all the melodic extensions of the model and the possibilities of the algorithm's interpretation tools, we will now analyze how this can be extended and we will also interpret consonances and progressions thus harmony structures. We'll start with the two-part counterpoint study.

Let us see whether the rhetoric is affected considering the information we're getting from a progression, in the case of parallel movements of two-part voicings.

Each of these progressions matches A's rhetoric which refers to a comma as it is a major 2nd ascending (see punctuation marks index). What differs is the feeling of each resonance as the vertical intervals change in each case.

The same applies to all parallel movements. The rhetoric of the progression of consonances depends on the melodic interval of the base and not on the vertical intervals. We supported from the beginning that the function of melody differs in relation to that of chords and harmonic progression.

The rhetoric of harmonic progression is a concept that includes the information we get from melody and chords, combined.

But if we don't confine ourselves to the interpretation of parallel movements only, what do we get? Let's see what happens to some chord progressions that tonal music has noted as cadences and have specific rhetoric.

A		B		C		D	
G	C	G	Cm	G	C	D⁷	G

major 2nd ascending   minor 2nd ascending   tied note   major 2nd descending

minor 2nd ascending   minor 2nd ascending   major 2nd ascending   tied note

tied note   tied note   minor 2nd ascending   minor 2nd descending

                                                 perfect 5th descending   minor 2nd ascending

                                                                   perfect 4th ascending

In the cases above, we chose some connections that are all characterized as perfect cadences. The perfect cadence has a rhetoric which corresponds to the full-stop in speech.

A) In this case, we have three movements. The tied note does not affect the rhetoric of the connection as we have seen in our analyses in relation to speech punctuation marks. The ascending major 2nd is common in the case of comma and the semicolon. The ascending minor 2nd is a typical full-stop. So, we can say that even if we didn't know that this was a perfect cadence, we could imagine the rhetoric of this connection. Perhaps it isn't in its strongest form but certainly is a definite full-stop thus a perfect cadence sounding progression.

B) Three simultaneous movements again. The difference in the case of A is that instead of the major 2nd, we have another minor 2nd ascending. Our model would again characterize the rhetoric of this connection as affirmative (thus a perfect cadence sounding one) and rather stronger than the previous one.

C) Same case of intervals as A, with an extra perfect 5th descending. Therefore, the rhetoric that refers to a full-stop intensifies because the descending perfect 5th is classified in the intervals that belong to the rhetoric of the period (full-stop).

46

D) The intervals of minor 2nd ascending and perfect 4th ascending are intervals classified as period. The tied note does not affect the rhetoric of the progression. The minor 2nd descending belongs to the intervals of the full-stop column although not in the strong ones and the major 2nd descending belongs to the full-stop as well. So, with so many affirmative intervals, we would be sure that this progression projects a very strong full-stop rhetoric (again a perfect cadence).

Let's look at how other progressions are interpreted by the model.

A		B		C		D	
G	D	G	D	G	D⁷	Gmaj⁷	D⁷

tied note
major 2nd descending
minor 2nd descending

major 3rd ascending
major 2nd descending
perfect 4th descending

perfect 4th descending
major 2nd descending
major 2nd descending
minor 2nd descending

tied note
tied note
major 2nd descending
major 2nd ascending
major 2nd descending

All cases of the image are characterized as half cadences. They give a sense of a need to hear that something follows, a feeling of uncertainty.

A) The tied note does not affect the rhetoric of the progression, like all repetitions do. The major 2nd descending belongs to the rhetoric of the comma and the minor one to the full-stop (but not of the strong cases). We would say that the sense of the comma dominates but not decisively.

B) The major 3rd ascending belongs to the question mark's rhetoric. The major 2nd descending belongs to the full-stop column but not in the strong cases and the perfect 4th descending in the same category. We would, therefore, say that the question mark is to prevail, but since it is accompanied by two (not very strong) intervals of the full-stop column, it is likely that the result will be a sense towards comma (comma belongs to the intervals of 3rd, but not in the strong ones).

C) Similarly, we have 3 intervals of non-strong full-stops and a minor 2nd descending which belongs to the very weak full-stops. We are therefore expecting a very uncertain outcome.

D) Tied notes do not affect the progression. The major 2nds descending create a sense of non-strong full-stop while the major 2nd ascending is a strong comma. We, therefore, expect an uncertain ending feeling, while at the same time a strong hint that something needs further continuation.

A	B	C	D
major 2nd ascending	major 2nd ascending	minor 2nd descending	major 2nd ascending
minor 2nd ascending	major 2nd descending	major 2nd descending	major 2nd ascending
major 2nd ascending	minor 2nd ascending	major 2nd ascending	minor 2nd ascending
	major 2nd ascending	minor 2nd ascending	minor 2nd descending
			major 2nd descending

All the links above are classified as interrupted cadences. One affirmative connection but not as strong as a perfect one (full-stop).

A) The major 2nds ascending belong to the comma column while the minor 2nd ascending to the period. The combination gives an affirmative result with, at the same time, an intense element of need to continue.

B) Likewise, here, with the difference that a major 2nd descending was added, an interval that refers to full-stop. Similar rhetoric with a slight reinforcement of the affirmative tension. This may consist of a reason to double the 3rd of the VI on V-VI progressions, this particular note is the tonic of the scale and thus strengthens the sense of return to the tonal center.

C) Here, a major 2nd ascending was replaced with a minor 2nd descending, an interval that refers again to a full-stop rhetoric but not a strong one. Similar rhetoric.

D) Here, we also have similar rhetoric as a major 2nd ascending, interval of the comma column has been added, slightly reinforcing the need for continuation.

A	B	C	D
major 3rd ascending	major 2nd ascending	major 2nd descending	minor 3rd ascending
major 2nd descending	tied note	tied note	minor 2nd descending
perfect 4th descending	major 2nd descending	major 2nd ascending	major 2nd ascending
	major 3rd ascending	minor 2nd descending	tied note

The connections above are characterized as plagal cadences. This type of cadence gives a sense of closure but in a softer way than the perfect cadence, not so decisively.

A) The major 3rd ascending is a question mark interval. The major 2nd descending is a full-stop, as is the perfect 4th descending. These two intervals are less dynamic than the first, so we expect that their combination will be affirmative with a sense of question distorting the listening.

B) The major 2nd ascending is a comma, the tied note does not affect the progression rhetoric, the major 2nd descending is a full-stop of moderate power and the major 3rd ascending is a strong question mark. We would say that the combination of all the above would be similar to the effect of the case A.

C) This case falls short of any intervals of 3rd and instead, we get a minor 2nd descending that strengthens the affirmative rhetoric.

D) The minor 3rd ascending is also a question mark interval, of lesser determination than the major 3rd though. The major 2nd ascending produces the sense of comma while the minor 2nd descending of a lesser full-stop. Overall, we expect that our feeling about the progression will be a little more uncertain than the A case but with similarities.

We see that the model not only agrees with the establishments of tonal music but enters deeper, providing the possibility of a more detailed examination of progressions. The intervallic combinations can be evaluated by the composer using the algorithm, giving him/her the power to act independently of the tonality, knowing in advance the subtle nuances that make up every progression. Something which, until recently, could be known only through experimentation, in order for the composer to be able to imagine what a progression would sound like. GMT provides an established ground knowledge through the algorithm, because of our familiarization with emotions and punctuation, conveyed through speech.

In the cases of cadences, we had a perfect match with the rhetoric attributed to them, through the doctrine of traditional harmony and GMT, but we could see also the extent to which one structure or the other serves better our rhetoric needs, through its combinational rhetoric of melodic interval of the chords separately.

Well-known harmonic errors could well be described as redundant elements which distort the intended rhetoric, as they do not give anything new to a progression. They are only a means of giving emphasis on specific melodic movements.

Non-chord tones

Non-chord tones, an integral component of harmonic thinking, can be integrated into the model if we think of them in a more abstract way, meaning that we will need to define them in a way that will not be dependent on the limited model of traditional harmony but will apply in any harmonic environment.

With the term "non-chord tone" we describe all those notes that we cannot justify as ones that belong in a specific chord.

This implies that it is consistent with various rules of conduct of these notes and their classification as well as some common general features.

Common characteristics of non-chord tones:

Their duration must be equal or less than that of the consonant notes.

We will see a number of cases where some notes are clearly non-chord tones, but they may last longer than the ones who are considered as consonant. We must take into account the style of the music in which we have located them and their place in the overall harmony.

Practically, they should be of equal or less duration than the average of the rhythmic values that are within the effect of the same chord for psychoacoustic reasons. If the non-chord tone has exceeded this analogy then it should justify its role as a stylistic commonality. If the listener has no familiarity with this particular style it will lead him/her to consider the non-chord tone as a part of the chord, which negates its role.

By identifying the harmonic rhythm (the time that a chord lasts, regardless of the rhythmic values) we can define the total duration of a chord, and then we can divide this duration by the total number of notes belonging in the melody within this duration. This way we find the average, which is often not obvious, and therefore we can control more accurately the outcome of the partnership of non-chord tones and consonant ones in relation to the desired harmonic background.

For example, in the following measure 4/4 we have 6 notes. This means that the average duration (if we consider that the passage belongs to a single chord) is 4/4 to 6, i.e. 1/6. As a rhythmic value, 1/6 does not exist in music unless we take a note out of a quarter sextuplet. 1/6 it is a little larger than 1/8 and a little less than 1/4 so in the example below we know that if we don't want the non-chord tone that we wrote, to be heard as part of the chord that accompanies our melody, it shouldn't be the quarter or the dotted quarter of the passage, but it may be the eighth or some note of the triplet of eighths.

In the following example, the total duration remains the same but the number of notes has changed. So, we get an average duration of 1/8. This shows us that, in this situation, whether a note is capable of being considered a candidate for a non-chord tone does not depend so much on how long it lasts, as most of the durations here are eighths.

We can predict how diatonic or chromatic progression will be received by the listener, with no limitation on how many simultaneous parts we have (counter-melodies). This element, as we mentioned above, relates only to the amount of information we want to introduce in our harmony as well as to the level of complexity of our harmonic environment.

More examples of harmonic progressions

After referring to the non-chord tones, let us return to the study of progressions, based on our model, and specifically what we derive from our knowledge of the punctuation marks.

Let's look at some examples of a variety of material:

A	B	C	D
minor 6th ascending	minor 2nd ascending	minor 2nd descending	major 3rd descending
minor 3rd ascending	major 2nd descending	tied note	minor 3rd ascending
	perfect 4th ascending	minor 3rd ascending	tied note
		major 2nd ascending	major 2nd ascending
			diminished 4th descending

A) The minor 6th ascending is a negative exclamatory interval. The minor 3rd is a negative question mark. Therefore, the rhetoric of the progression is expected to cause us a sense of question and admiration at the same time (perhaps a very energetic question) with a negative connotation. If we judge it in terms of its emotional content, it ranks in the emotion of Astonishment.

B) All intervals have been chosen to induce the rhetoric of a full-stop.

C) We see in turn from top to bottom, a weak full-stop, an indifferent interval, a negative question mark and a strong comma. We expect a negative emotional outcome with dominant the element for continuation.

D) We see in turn, a negation, a strong question mark with a negative tendency, an indifferent interval, a strong comma and an interval that sounds like a major 3rd descending thus a negation. Our overall assessment is that this consonance will probably refer to a sense of negation with a sad question that needs to be answered.

Of course, in this method of progression analysis, we must include a factor which is related to the amount of information we receive. There is already a very useful tool with this capability, and this is the Hindemith[1] chord classification system, which is about chord tension. This classification gives us the estimated root of each consonance and its place on an axis that actually represents the degree of complexity of harmony. This latter factor can be said to be proportional to the Energy we can give to a chord and inversely proportional to its Positivity. It is, therefore, a thorough method of evaluating a chord in reference to the axes of the Energy and Positivity of our two-axis plane. The tension-diagram of a progression resulting from this analysis can be combined with the other methods of controlling the rhetoric we propose, to have a controlled effect on the tension of a progression.

The values we receive from the Hindemith analysis, always refer to the tension of the chord. They are values that relate to emotional tension. The mood, however, is directly influenced by the connection of the chords (the progression), whose method of control of the rhetoric we analyzed above. Complex chord constructions have a root as well, and one can (if he/she connects the roots of chords in a progression) define the rhetoric, relating to micro-energic differences, as they would do by analyzing the connection of degrees in harmony.

There is no particular meaning in the characterization of the emotional contents of a chord as it is not enough to identify with a particular emotion. It's a summary of a melody. The melody through its mobility reveals the meaning of the content's story, revealing emotion and overall mood. The chord gives us a concentrated feeling of abstract emotional content that looks more like a fleeting perception of a situation. Chord progression is the melodic collaboration of many chords, resulting in having the highest amount of information.

It is important, for a chord, to be defined in terms of complexity. Its connection with other chords is the one that will eventually form the impression of the progression's mood which will be the bearing mechanism in the construction of a composition.

---

1. Paul Hindemith – *The Craft of Musical Composition*

Only between chords of the same Hindemith classification (or a newer classification that incorporates them to the same degree in terms of psychological tension), one can distinguish the degree of their relative Positivity. Anything different is quite difficult and possibly the transition from one level of complexity to another is harder to be defined compared to the individual building materials of each chord. In case we are talking about the same classification of chords, we can identify the degree of Positivity of its content based on the interval distribution in relation to the root (taking into account the lists of positive or negative intervals of the model, although they are considered to be melodic intervals).

E.g.
Among the three-part chords:

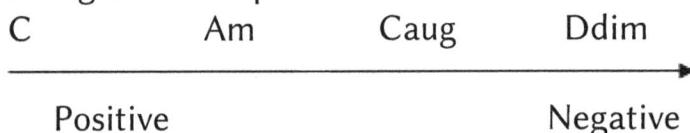

C	Am	Caug	Ddim

Positive → Negative

E.g.
Among 7th chords :

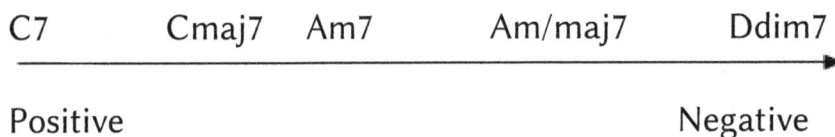

C7	Cmaj7	Am7	Am/maj7	Ddim7

Positive → Negative

and so on...

(This is simply an estimation of their distribution on this axis, each composer, of course, may have his/her own opinion on the subject. The estimation was made based on the type and amount of positive or negative intervals from the root they contain)

In the case of complex chords, their analysis based on the theories relating to the harmonic series will allow us to find their estimated root. It is considered that each interval has a root, as very aptly observed in the book by Antonis I. Antonopoulos, *From tonality to contemporary music theory*. We estimate that natural acoustic properties were incorporated in the expression of speech through the evolution of humankind. This allows us to calculate how high or low each chord has been transferred in relation to the previous one (since their microtonicity is something indicative) and to find the apparent displacement of the energy center of the chord, which is related to the Energy axis of our model, thus making useful correlations. Then we can do a corresponding ranking based on the intervals they contain and come up with a more complete tension-chart. As long as we are close to the tonal harmony the minimum and maximum energy levels are defined by the rhetoric of the degrees as we perceive them through the study of traditional harmony (e.g. I is the most inert, the V the one with the greatest instability, etc.). The more we distance ourselves from this approach, the less efficient is the use of the bipole of I and V as a way of evaluating psychological tension. The 5th degree is not anymore the tone with the highest energy as the rules resulting from the algorithm of tonal harmony have gradually ceased to exist. The intervals and the notes on which the intervals are leading the melody, as microtonicity points, acquire a distinct and broader dynamic which is calculated with the help of our model. We shall see more practically how this can be done in a more abstract harmonic environment (we will give an example in the next chapter).

With the help of the aforementioned, we can classify kinds of harmonic tension on an axis related to their complexity. The endorsement of chords through their ranking into families that concern their psychological tension, could inform us if we are in close or distant areas in terms of stylistic consistency when we use a variety of harmonic structures.

For example, the triads that do not contain tritones belong to the lowest class of complexity (or as Hindemith would define, belong to the most powerful harmonic chords). The harmony of the classical period would be at this level of complexity with the exception of the V7 and the rarest appearances of diminished chords belonging to the second class level of Hindemith. On the next level, we're getting into the harmony of romanticism (but also jazz and other types of music that make use of the same level of complexity), where it becomes more common to use dissonant intervals in chords (without necessarily requiring their solution) like the minor 7th and the major 2nd. At the next level, we have the incorporation of major 7th and minor 2nd in chords (most often encountered in works of the twentieth century) and in the last two levels, we see undefined chords and the tritone prevailing (as opposed to the second level where the tritones are subordinated to the other intervals). We can match the class of chords (and by extension the harmonies that use them) to an axis related to complexity, which is the psychological tension created by the sense of uncertainty and predictability of the harmonic content:

The psychological tension is proportional to the complexity

———————————————————————————————————————▶

This classification is consistent with our model as the intensity of the vertical interval usage is proportional to the complexity of the melodies of all the independent voices. The latter ones are characterized by the intervals they use melodically and as we saw in the parallelism of tonal music and the model before, the more complicated the rhetoric of intervals, considering the punctuation they represent, also harmony tends to move to a higher Hindemith class.

Also, regardless of the contrapuntal approach, the chords can be controlled by the model if we consider that the intervals have a rhetoric related to the microtonicity (of a small melodic excerpt– like a spoken word for example). Therefore, the bass note of a chord is taken as the tonal center from which we draw conclusions about the rhetoric of the above-stated notes.

For example, if we have a consonance that contains a 3rd, then we hear something that points to a question mark. If we add a 2nd from the root, we will simultaneously have 2 intervals representing commas (from the root to the 2nd and from the 2nd to the 3rd) and a question interval (the 3rd from the root). This complicates the listening as it complicates the rhetoric as well. The rhetoric of the consonants must be combined with the rhetoric of the melodic movement in order to achieve the greatest possible control of our material.

Let us make another example where we have a major chord. If we analyze it with our model, we hear a happy question mark from the root and a sad one from the 3rd (since the 3rd of the chord is a major one and its distance from the perfect 5th is a minor 3rd). At the same time, we hear the perfect 5th from the root, an interval of exclamation. So the intervals from our root compose a happy question mark and an exclamation mark, while the minor 3rd from the 3rd to the 5th is not perceived as a significant interval in the specific consonance, because it doesn't start from the same root. The sad question mark of this interval merely helps as a question mark on the overall sense of the joyful question-exclamation and wonderous sentiment expression of the major chord.

This is why students often get confused when they hear a first inversion of a major chord and mistake it for minor, as the bass first forms a minor 3rd with the note above (i.e. from the 3rd of the chord to the 5th). The interval from the bass to the highest note is a minor 6th, which gives the sensation of a sad exclamation and finally the interval from the 5th of the chord to the root (the octave of the root), is a perfect 4th which is affirmative. So in total, we hear something sad.

Another problem that one may encounter in acoustic dictation exercises is that while the student can detect the type of a chord easily when listening to it alone, usually in a progression they get confused. Experience shows that this depends very much on the interval that the roots of the chords are apart. If, for example, we hear an A minor chord and then a B♭ major, the distance between them (the roots) is minor 2nd, an interval that belongs to the negative intervals and therefore sometimes confuses the overall sensation by giving a negative tinge that the novice confuse with the minor chord-type that are already accustomed with and identify it with this sensation.

Therefore, the rhetoric of progression is directly related to the melodic movement between the notes and the vertical distribution of intervals (from the bass), thus outlining a synergy of the axis of storytelling of the melody with that of emotion (which is carried mainly by the chords) and of the mood (carried by the connection of chords) showing a transition from the musical microcosm to the macrocosm through analogy. We should mention at this point that Set Theory is particularly useful for the handling of intervals in melodic movements and therefore the applications of our model. Through Set Theory the intervals can be simplified as distances from a zero point and get values according to the half steps they include.

More contemporary theories for the evaluation of complex chords start from the triads and reach up to the 12tone vertical structures. Then we have the categories of chords with added notes, chords with overlayed intervals of 2nds or 4ths or 5ths, polychords, complex chords, harmonic constructions with various architectures, clusters, etc. Through what we mentioned about consonance and its evaluation with the GMT, we can draw parallel conclusions and enrich our training.

The psychological tension is related to the positive or negative intervals as well as to all other factors of our model. For example, let's take the factor of Pitch accuracy. Pitch accuracy is the tendency to choose very specific and delineate notes (which seems more clearly when notes are repeated within a passage and show consistency in choosing the note accurately). So, we can derive as a conclusion that singing, which by definition is a state of speech that has great Pitch accuracy (thus this is a desideratum) is generally more positive than the usual speech. Hence the pleasantness in the pronunciation of Italians.

An example of a reduction in Positivity (and thus an increase in psychological tension) is what follows, where the reader will notice a transition from a state of controlled glissando, chromaticism and very low dynamics, to a situation where we see glissando simultaneously with vibrato, microtonal intervals and higher dynamics.

(excerpt from a composition of the author)

The aim of this two-bar excerpt is to increase the psychological tension and the second violin to be distinguishable when the passage reaches a small climax. This is why the second violin is the only one that does not show any differentiation in microtonicity. Another factor is the change in the position of the bow (from s.p. – sul ponticello to ord.) as we move towards a more endearing acoustic quality in the sound of the string instrument, thus increasing the attention of the listener.

The tension of chords

In addition to the models already proposed in the past to assess the psychological tension of chords, the speech model provides its own perspective on the subject.

Speech has incorporated our inherent biological knowledge of the harmonic series. But while speech is a melodic and not a vertical view of sound, it can be extended through another biological heritage, the acoustic memory.

The acoustic memory is responsible for the fact that we can recognize a melodic interval (if this is not the result of a perfect pitch, which is rare). We remember the note we heard because we need to compare it with the next one and draw a conclusion about the interval between them. This melodic interval is, in fact, a phantom harmonic interval because while we hear the current note, we remember the previous one. There is, therefore, a relationship between the harmonic intervals and the melodic ones. In our model, the ease of evaluation of consonances lies in the fact that each interval relates to both emotional information (positive or negative) and rhetorical information that has to do with the point of punctuation that it represents.

While we hear a harmonic interval, emotional information is more tangible because both notes are present and this has effects on our hearing organ. For example, a dissonant interval such as the perfect 4th ascending equals to a full-stop, in our model. If the two notes of the interval are heard simultaneously (harmonic interval) we receive again the same information (as the melodic interval provides us) but the fact that we continue to listen to the bass note creates a physical effect on our drum which is clearly more pronounced than what we would have we were just listening to the conclusion of the melodic interval (the 4th above the bass), and remember only the bass. The positivity or negativity of the intervals affects tension if seen this way.

Through the model, we can assess tension by analyzing the simultaneous punctuation marks that are created by the harmonic intervals from the bass.

• • • • • • • •

Analysis

Let's take as example a simple consonance

The melodic interval of minor 7th ascending indicates a semicolon. If we play the minor 7th as a harmonic interval (thus both notes simultaneously), we find that it continues to give us the same feeling.

If we add a note then we have two intervals starting from the same root.

One interval is still the minor 7th and a minor 3rd from E is added. The latter corresponds to a sad question based on the model. This means according to what we said in the acoustic memory argument, that we will now receive the rhetorical information of a sad question along with the semicolon. If we play this chord we will see (at least this happens in my personal acoustic assessment) that we receive these two rhetorical elements simultaneously without causing any particular tension.

I believe that the criterion for assessing the psychological tension of a chord is the level of meaning-accordance of the rhetoric elements (punctuation) that we receive from each interval separately.

That means that if these two punctuation marks can stand at the same time in an imaginary situation, as an expressive need, etc. then they will create a consonance with an acoustic tension commensurate with the psychological tension that we will receive if we handle the respective cognitive meanings of these meaning vectors. If two or more punctuation marks begin to not be able to stand together, then this starts to create a tension of the level of psychological pressure derived from hearing this consonance. Let's look at some examples and their evaluations.

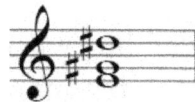

major 3rd => happy question
major 7th => intense question

It is a consonance without much tension as the meanings of the intervals' rhetoric are consistent with each other (questions). At the same time, it is a stable chord as the root, which is the tonic -one octave above- (2nd harmonic in the harmonic series), provides less intensely the solution of the interval of the major 7th, reducing somewhat the efficacy of the question mark. The 3rd is the one that validates the fact of the E = root, and thus ensures us that the 7th seeks its solution to the next E.

major 3rd => happy question
minor 7th => semicolon

If we combine the meanings of the intervals above, I think we will agree that they fit the sound of the dominant 7th chord and its role as we knew it in traditional harmony. It is, therefore, an analysis of the meaning of a V7 (omitting the fifth of the chord).

minor 2nd => full-stop
diminished 5th => interval which can fit all punctuation marks (and full-stop also) but not with great effectiveness

A sense of full-stop is produced but with an enigmatic connotation as we will see. This happens often when the tritone is involved but in this case, another reason is involved too, the fact that not all the intervals here have the same root if we analyze them based on what we learned about interval roots with the help of the harmonic series. The F – B♭ has as root B♭ and this intensifies the complexity of the consonance and thus the psychological tension increases.

We can simplify the acoustic outcome of the chord by analyzing it to those roots of intervals. We need to do that so that in the end we see one single final interval that is formed through this process of root elimination. For example, one interval has a root, let's call it root A and another one has a root, root B; we can find the main root by identifying the root of the interval A - B.

Here, if we make this simplification, we receive E as the one root and B♭ as a second; the final result is the interval that these two non-final roots form which is an enigmatic mark. In this case, we will incorporate it into the sense of the full-stop as this advocates its constituent intervals.

Therefore, we observe that a classification of chords can be easily done in any harmonic environment, without limitation to the number of notes in a consonance, by extending the method above (of correlation between intervals and punctuation), seeing them vertically (harmoniously). Perhaps it is best that the composer chooses the course of psychological tension in their work in a way that their overall harmony can be integrated into one stylistic manner. If this is not something they desire, they can always control the tension of the harmony, so in conjunction with the rhetoric of connections they can achieve the desired outcome for the composition, regardless of stylistic limitations.

We also have to add that the chords can change their position on the axis of psychological tension if we alter the pitch accuracy of the notes we choose in a passage. In this way the distances between the notes stop being divided into semitones or even quartertones and cover all the intermediate areas, considering (in contrast to the digitalization given by the quantum quality of the notion of dividing the octave into specific ratios) the "grey areas" between tones.

The psychological intensity of a chord is the result of all the factors that we have used in relation to the pitch height, creating proportions in a way that is predictable by the model, considering that this psychological tension is proportional to Energy and the Emphasis and is inversely proportional to Positivity.

Two of the most important elements of the evaluation of the rhetoric of a whole passage or even of a whole composition are the axes of **Duration** and **Volume**.

A passage, whose average duration of the values alters, causes a direct alteration of the uptake of its Energy by the listener. For example, a motif that starts quickly and ends slowly causes a sense of shifting from energetic emotions to passive ones. The same thing happens when we have a whole theme which is quick and slows down, and of course, all the other combinations of our model apply too. In the same way, the volume factor is very important. The rhetoric includes the axis of positivity but it is determined by the parameters that we analyzed earlier, which relate to how the notion of mood in a passage or entire work is finally formed.

Speech, in this way, has given us tools for every dimension of music. It can tell a story through its melodic aspect, it can create instant emotions through the consonances and chords but it also can control the overall mood of a musical work through the manipulation of harmony and relation of chords in progressions.

● ● ● ● ● ● ● ●

Synthesis

Tension analysis in progressions

Let's say we have a given harmonic progression and we want to analyze it:

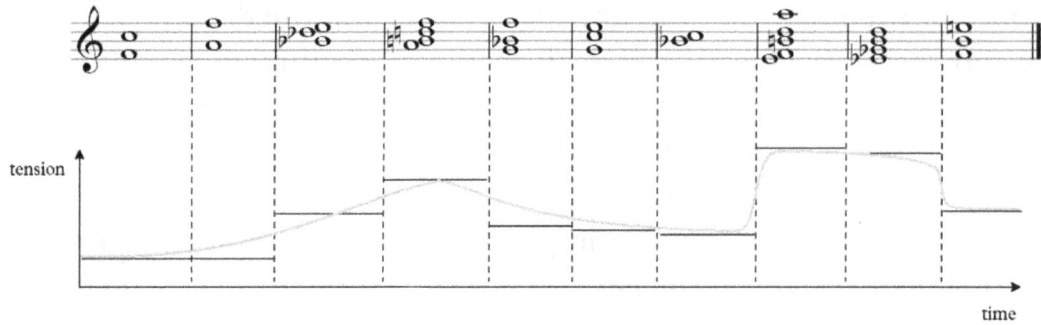

In the vertical axis we've set the psychological tension and in the horizontal the time. The levels noted are based on comparisons of tensions between the chords of the progression we are examining. The height at which they are marked does not have an objective validation of any short but the hierarchy of differences between them is clearly defined through the process of the chord-tension evaluation we already described.

In order to have a complete progression study, we should look at the above along with information of the orchestration to draw conclusions about the overall emotional variations as it is influenced through all the 7 columns of the algorithm. For example, it is clear that variations in Volume will have a direct impact on psychological tension.

Let's suppose that we are talking about a progression in which these factors remain stable and the only thing that changes is harmony. To have a full picture of the effect of the progression, we need to know the rhetoric of connections as we have seen before; the speech-based model has the tools to analyze chord connections based on the rhetoric of the melodic connection of each note and not only roughly by recognizing the role of each chord in a limited algorithm such as traditional harmony.

If we want a more cursory reading of the intensity of the progression, we can limit the need to detect the rhetoric of melodic movements of the notes by observing only the root of each chord and then evaluate their rhetoric as a bass melody. This way we can have an idea of the sense of punctuation implied by the harmony that is superpositioned.

Applications in improvisation

Having analyzed issues related to composition using the model, we can easily move on to how this can be applied as an improvisation tool.

A problem lies in the fact that in improvisation we don't have much time to process our data. We will, therefore, limit our material to the required degree.

If we improvise in a tonal environment, then our necessary data background must be the chords of the progression on which we improvise. With the knowledge of scale and arpeggios, we can draw ideas from our model in order to make melodies.

At first, we can use the index with punctuation marks. These can give us the necessary tools to know when the ending of a phrase we play is affirmative, questioning, exclamatory, etc. and to what extent. These intervals (of the index of punctuation marks) can be used both melodically and harmonically. This means that in our melodic approach, when we go from one note to another, we know how to predict the meaning that is implied by our rhetoric of the melody we improvise. But because we have a tonal center and we are not completely free, the feeling we get from listening to the notes we play in relation to the accompaniment, plays an equally important role in the overall rhetoric. If our notes have equal duration to the harmonious pace (one note in melody per chord) then we must think of them as part of the harmony, but if they tend to be smaller, then we are led to the increase of the importance of the melodic intervals of the transition from note to note. Always the root of the chord will be the target of a full-stop, while the relationship with the other harmonic intervals will determine whether the rhetoric of the note we play corresponds to a comma, question mark, etc. Obviously, good knowledge of arpeggios along with the practice leads to being able to identify all kinds of intervals (of the index) within the harmony and this will allow us to choose the appropriate intervals each time to achieve the desired rhetoric result.

For example, let's suppose that our accompaniment consists of a G minor chord only. Knowing the scale and the arpeggios, we can choose the appropriate notes to melodically produce a punctuation mark. Let's say we want to produce a question mark, this means that if a note is long and we consider it to be integrated into harmony, it's better to choose the B♭, which is brought to the surface by the timbre of our instrument and because it is the minor 3rd of the chord; it sounds like a sad question. If we wanted an exclamation mark we should do the same with the 5th of the chord, namely D.

We can melodically use all the intervals of the index, with smaller rhythmic values so the melodic line produces a more distinct message and differentiates from harmony. So if we want to make a full-stop, we can move towards the root of the chord (G) from F# with a minor 2nd ascending, from A with major 2nd descending, from the D with a perfect 4th ascending or perfect 5th descending but also from the F natural with a major 2nd ascending because even though it's not a strong full-stop interval the sense of the ending on the root will overcome the inadequacy of the melodic interval.

Likewise, we can do the same towards the other notes of the arpeggio but also, in the case of a chord change, towards the notes of the arpeggio of the chord that follows. The knowledge of modal and other types of scales related to the harmony helps us even more in predicting the overall feeling that we will get from these approaches to the notes of chords as the micromodality created over the harmony of every chord is part of the overall rhetoric in macroscopic analysis and we should be able to predict it.

In case the harmonic material expands, the same thing happens with the amount of the consonant notes and thus of our melodic freedom. In an absolutely atonal environment, we will, therefore, have marginally the freedom to think only of melodic intervals and thus our punctuation marks, and we will not have to worry about their place in the harmony because the latter will be weakened noticeably.

We saw in a previous chapter that accompaniment can be considered anything between one note and the totality of the available notes. The distribution of the chords as we proposed in relation to their tension will inform us about the level of the coherence of the progression, as we will have a reference point about when we have incomplete or lacking harmonic Information, when it's sufficient and when it's excessive or unclear.

Technological applications of the model

A model can always help with practical applications in technology, as this makes the data we receive, measurable and therefore manageable.

Applications in the field of technology through the use of computer capabilities and computing can be achieved, using the model for various needs.

Depending on what we seek we can put a set of automated processes in order to use the model and have a useful output.

The two main approaches we propose are related to two needs on a technical aspect. One is the adequate recognition of human emotion in speech and the other is the reproduction of speech with sufficiency and precision in the method that is used by the synthetic voice of computers, in order to achieve a more natural means of expression than the current, machine learning methods.

The ways in which such an application can be achieved are many; all we can provide in the context of the book is important diagrams for these two general categories of application in the field of technology.

Schematic diagram for emotion recognition:

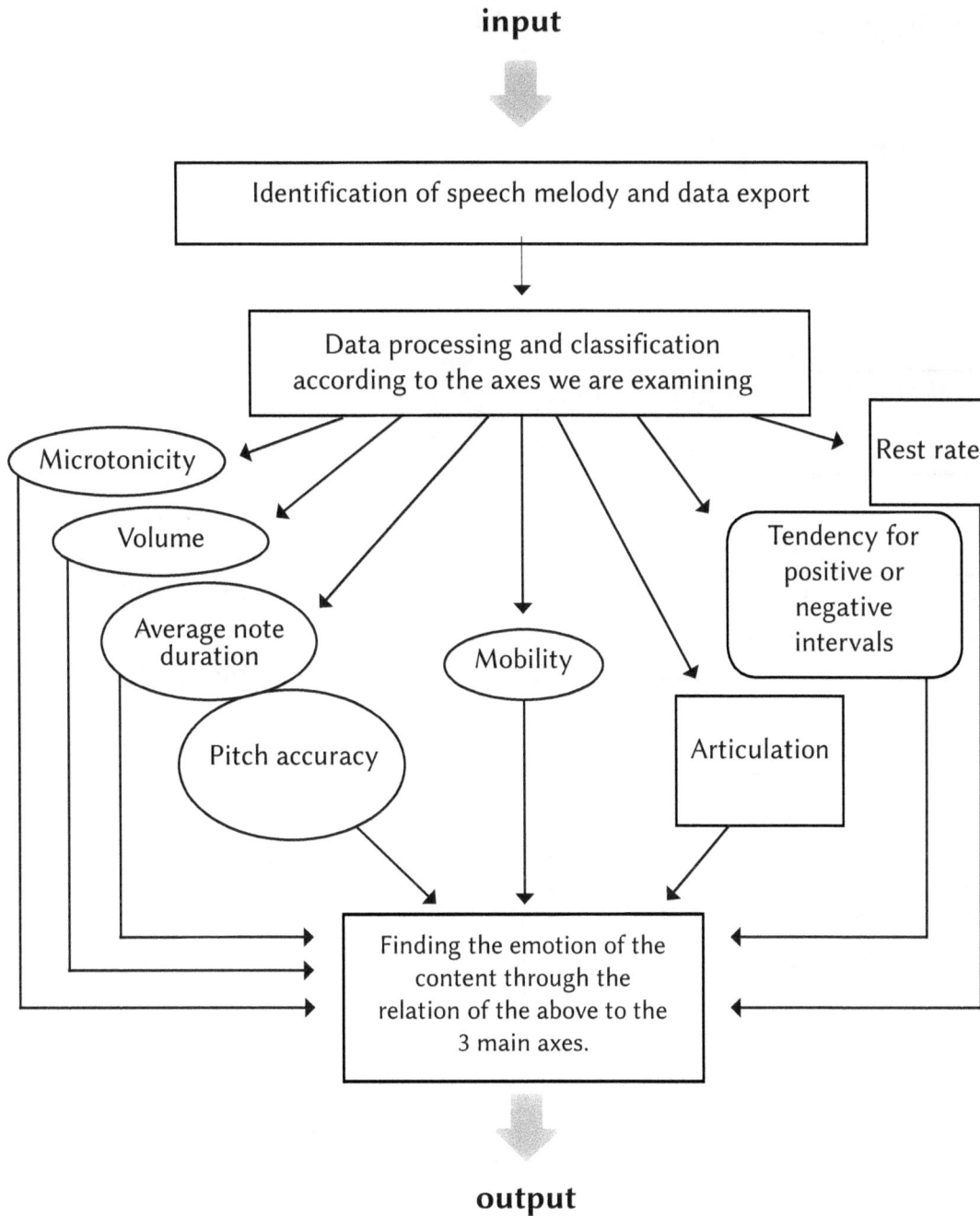

input

Identification of speech melody and data export

Data processing and classification according to the axes we are examining

Microtonicity

Rest rate

Volume

Tendency for positive or negative intervals

Average note duration

Mobility

Pitch accuracy

Articulation

Finding the emotion of the content through the relation of the above to the 3 main axes.

output

Some experimental adjustments are necessary for calibration so that the connective settings of the factors are functional and efficient. This is where artificial intelligence can be of service. Let us proceed now to a schematic representation of the application of the creation of synthetic speech with accurate emotional content.

Synthetic voice schematic:

Phrase input

Digital analysis of the grammatical elements of the phrase

Distributor of the semantic priority of the elements of the phrase

Identification of the hierarchy of the words, by their importance

Classier of values from the list of dependent factors based on estimates of the Energy, Positivity and Emphasis resulting from the input of emotion

Input of the emotion associated with the phrase

Distributor of intervals for the punctuation marks

List of values output to synthetic voice editor and then to

Explanations and notes for the schematic diagram

1st distributor:

It defines which word is more important than the other because this will play a role when importance needs to be matched with a certain microtonicity and volume.

Hierarchy of words:

Identifying the subject, the verb, some adverbs, pronouns, etc. This will be done by some kind of artificial intelligence in case it happens automatically, which determines which words have greater significance than others, which has the maximum, which are indifferent etc.

Classier:

The 7 quantities that are attached to our model (Volume, Mobility, Vibrato, Pitch accuracy, Articulation, Duration, Rest rate). Each word acquires its own "coordinates" of values from these lists as the classification of words gave a semantic priority list. The latter affects the displacement of the average duration of notes in some direction, as the mood of the phrase is set by the emotion chosen as input, but the relative deviations of the words from it are influenced by the significance of each word separately within the phrase.

2nd distributor:

These syllables are the accented ones and the ones with punctuation marks (at least semantically).

For example, defining what is most important in the phrase. The subject, the verb, some adverbs, pronouns, etc. This will be done by some kind of artificial intelligence, in case it is automated, which determines which words have greater significance than others in the phrase, which has the maximum significance, which are indifferent, etc.

Conclusion

The model we analyzed resulted from many experiments and analyses and the part we present in the book is only the necessary part so that we do not tire the reader with technical details and statistical results. We also don't want to tire with other proposals for applications that can be made, such as in acting by learning the correct expression of speech in order to express emotion, directing, dancing, psychology evaluations through speech analysis, etc. The GMT model seems to be inexhaustible in this field and here we wanted to focus only on the use of it as a method to re-learn music, a method for composition and analysis, as a guide for performance and as a critique tool.

The outcome of this approach, in addition to fulfilling a need for finding a method that gives answers to multiple rhetorical issues and the need to find an explanation for the existence of common grounds among the various musical systems, it is also the testimony of personal experience and experimentation of many decades.

I hope the experienced composer will find it useful and will receive a little more confidence in technical issues, while the student will use it as a personal growth and progress evaluation tool.

"When words fail,
music speaks"

Hans Christian Andersen

Bibliography

Andritsopoulos, M. (2017). *The Rhetoric of Music.* Athens: NAKAS.

Frankenhaeuser, M. (1974). Immediate and delayed effect of noise on performance and arousal, *Biological Psychology*, Vol.2,127-133.

Frangkos, G. (2007). *The "V-Transformer" VST plug-in: Changing the Vocal Effort of Human Singing Voice*, University of York, Departments of Electronics & Music.

Henkin, RI. (1963). Effect of sound on the hypothalamic-pituitary-adrenal axis, *Am. J. Physiol.*, Vol.204, 710-714.

Hindemith, P. (1990). *The craft of musical composition.* Translation K. Nasos, 2nd edition. Athens: Nasos.

Ilie, G. & Thompson, W. F. (2006). A Comparison of Acoustic Cues in Music and Speech for Three Dimensions of Affect, *Music Perception: An Interdisciplinary Journal*, Vol. 23 No. 4.

Kukreti, M. (2015). *Affective analysis of musical chords.* Conference Location: London

Lahdelma, I., & Eerola, T. (2016). Single chords convey distinct emotional qualities to both naïve and expert listeners. *Psychology of Music*, 44 (1), 37-54.

Nordstrom K. I. & Driessen P. F. (2006). Variable pre-emphasis LPC for modeling vocal effort in the singing voice, University of Victoria, Canada, *Conference on Digital Audio Effects (DAFx-06)*, Montreal, Canada, September 18-20.

Parrott, W. Gerrod (Ed.). (2001). Emotions in social psychology: essential readings. Philadelphia, PA: Psychology Press,

Plutchik, R., & Conte, H. R. (Eds.). (1997). *Circumplex models of personality and emotions.* Washington, DC, US: American Psychological Association.

Plutchik, R., & Kellerman, H. (1980). *Emotion: Theory, research and experience. Vol. 1, Theories of emotion.* New York: Academic Press.

Russell, J. A. (1980). A circumplex model of affect. *Journal of Personality and Social Psychology*, 39 (6), 1161-1178.

Shaver, P., Schwartz, J., Kirson, D., & O'Connor, C. (1987). Emotion knowledge: Further exploration of a prototype approach. *Journal of Personality and Social Psychology*, 52(6), 1061-1086.

Tomkins, S. S. (1962). *Affect imagery consciousness: Volume I, the positive affects.* London: Tavistock.

Tomkins, S. S. (1963). *Affect Imagery Consciousness: Volume II, the negative affects.* London: Tavistock.

www.ingramcontent.com/pod-product-compliance
Lightning Source LLC
Chambersburg PA
CBHW081239090426
42738CB00016B/3349